Table of Contents

1

Chapter 1:

The Case for Eliminating

Homework

"Parents are often so anxious about the consequences of their children no completing their homework, that I would say this is the number one source of stress for most families of school-age children I work with."

-   *Ruth Lazarus, Chicago Social Worker*

The Case for Eliminating Homework

Statement of the Problem

"If children are not required to learn useless and meaningless things, homework is entirely unnecessary for the learning of common school subjects. But when a school requires the amassing of many facts which have little or no significance to the child, learning is so slow and painful that the school is obliged to turn to the home for help out of the mess the school has created." (Carleton Washburn, school superintendent, *Parents* magazine, 1937)

The problem with homework as an educator put it is not that we should be asking how to do it but we should be asking why we are doing it. Alfie Kohn states is his book, <u>The Homework Myth: Why Our</u>

Kids Get Too Much of a Bad Thing, "The most striking trend regarding homework in the past two decades is the tendency to pile more and more of it on younger and younger children. The proportion of 6-8 year olds who are assigned homework is now almost the same as that for a 9-12 year old. In fact, homework is even becoming a routine part of the kindergarten experience." According to a 2004 report in *Teacher* magazine, "some parents say nightly assignments are too much of a strain on children who, not long ago, were still taking afternoon naps to make it through dinner."

In my experience as a teacher and a parent, the complaints about homework include stress on children, family conflict, less time for other enrichment activities, and a burden on parents.

1. **Stress on children**. Homework can be stressful for children in many ways. For example, it extends a workday that is already 8 hours long and for many children even longer due to after-school care. In 1938, America decided that a person working more than 40 hours a week posed a threat to adult health and productivity. Why shouldn't we use the same logic for school-age children? Much of the time students use to complete homework is time that could be used to allow them to relax and relieve anxieties from the school day. A hundred years ago, California outlawed homework because parents thought it was unhealthy for children, who were not getting an opportunity to play in fresh air and sunshine, things vital to good health.

2. **Family conflict**. Many parents have the same feeling that one family I spoke to concerning their 3 sons' homework load. They "dread it." How many parents end up arguing with their children over the way an assignment is supposed to be completed? How many become so frustrated with workload that they begin taking it out on the child instead of confronting the teacher and administration? Curt Dudley Marling, a professor at Boston College and former elementary school teacher, interviewed parents of children who were "slave learners." One father stated, "You end up ruining the relationship that you have with your kid." Another problem is that the talk of homework begins to dominate the evening discussion with questions like how much do you have and what do you have to do.

3. **Less time for enrichment activities**. This is a clear consequence of giving too much homework. As a parent of one of my students once told me, she can't teach her daughter how to cook their cultural food because her daughter has too much homework to do. Hobbies are great things for young people to have. It gives them the opportunity to find out more about themselves and things they are interested in so they can have well rounded lives.

4. **Burden on parents**. Annie Cassidy, author of Parents Who Think Too Much, poses an interesting question. "Are you listening to experts instead of trusting your instincts and your heart?" Many parents who struggle with homework question the validity of many of the

8

homework assignments their child is given. In
The End of Homework, authors Etta Kralovec
and John Buell state, "In education, this trend
(relying on experts) was reflected in the shift
away from parents and toward schools as the
primary socializing and educating entity."
When we send home science projects, book
reports, etc., we are assuming that parents can
help with these assignments when in reality we
may be setting some parents up for
embarrassment in front of their own children.
Many parents have too much respect to
confront a teacher or a school about this so the
cycle continues.

Recommendations of Practical Implementation

Some of the ways to eliminate or at least reduce the amount of homework our students are given are the following:

1. **Eliminate homework.** There are schools throughout the country that have decided that the negatives of homework outweigh the positives. One independent school in Colorado has taken this position and states in the book The Homework Myth, "6 ½ hours a day in school is enough. Kids and families need the rest of the days/weekends/holidays for living, playing, having friends and pets, shopping, solving problems, cooking, eating, (doing) chores, traveling, playing

10

on sports teams, communicating, finding out about world news, playing musical instruments, reading for pleasure, watching movies, collecting things, etc." For example, there is the story of 10-year-old Marie who wants to take dance lessons but since homework takes her 2-3 hours a day, she has no time.

2. **No homework for grades K-6.** Children at this age need to be able to develop social skills and problem-solving skills that don't come from homework but actually come from playing games or free play. As Piaget stated, "what work is to the adult, play is to the child." There is no statistical evidence that homework is beneficial for children in this age group. Harris Cooper, as educational psychologist, summarized the available research with a sentence that ought to be broadcast to every

parent, teacher, and administrator in the country: "There is no evidence that any amount of homework improves the academic performance of elementary students." Even Japan in the 1990's issued no homework policies.

3. **Make it hands-on.** As Rick Wormeli writes in his book <u>One Day & Beyond,</u> "Homework that is engaging is likely to be done. Break up routine homework with not-so-routine homework. Unique homework includes assignments that require students to interview family members or friends, incorporates artwork, music, drama, or media; and interacts with content and skill in meaningful ways."

4. **No homework on weekends and maximum of 2 nights per week.** Families deserve to be with their children on the weekends. Schools shouldn't be

dictating to families how any of their children's time in the late afternoons or evening must be spent. As educators, we often forget that in many situations we have both parents working 40 hours or more a week at least 5 days a week and many have things outside of schoolwork they want to teach their children on the weekends or weeknights or want their kids to participate in. This could include boy/girl scouts, recreation teams, cultural or religious group meetings, or sitting with a grandparent during the week.

In order to implement any of these ideas, leadership has to have the courage and influence to be able to enact a policy that does not follow the status quo. As Alfie Kohn states, "One reason we don't ask challenging questions about homework is that we don't ask challenging questions about most things." A leader (principal in this case) must ask and answer difficult questions concerning homework. If he/she has the trust of teachers and parents then he/she will be able to share their vision. An example of this is Christine Hendricks, the principal of Grant Elementary School in Glenrock, NY. Hendricks is also the mother of three children. In describing her daughter's experience in elementary school, she states, "by the fourth grade, she had so much homework, there was no time for after-school activities, playing, or simply enjoying our evenings together. We were always stressed, and I knew many other families were also miserable." Hendricks and her teachers looked into the research and decided to do an experiment and eliminate most homework with one exception – occasional studying for a test. "This is only the second year without it," she states, "but there have been no backslides in the classroom or IN TEST SCORES.

Parents say their kids enjoy reading again because there is no pressure. In fact, there have been no negative effects whatsoever." And there is much less stress at our home, too."

In Toronto, Canada, the Toronto School District adopted a new policy that affects more than 300,000 kids limiting homework to reading in elementary school, elementary holiday homework, and stating the value of family time. Here is the United States, the National Education Association (NEA) has a guideline that teachers should assign no more than 10 minutes per grade level per night so 10 minutes for a 1st grader, 20 minutes for a 2nd grader, etc.

These examples are in line with what one of our greatest scholars in the area of education and child-rearing, Imam Al-Ghazali, uses to describe the responsibilities of a teacher. According to Al-Ghazali, a teacher is one who "undertakes a great responsibility" and must treat the children as if they were his own children. We all want our children to have balanced lives. None of us want our kids to be what William Crain describes in his book <u>Reclaiming Childhood: Letting Children be Children on Our Achievement Oriented Society</u>. He states that, "we're seeing kids who are burned out by fourth grade. Soon it will be second grade."

Examples of Teachers and Schools Who Stopped Homework

There are many examples of teachers and schools that have decided that having a well-rounded life or at least be given that opportunity is much more important than doing homework. According to Alfie Kohn's <u>The</u>

Homework Myth, a father asked his 13-year old son whether he liked something he had just read. His son replied, "Well, it was a good book but I really never enjoy reading when I have an assignment hanging over my head." Mused the father, "Yup, that'll teach a lifelong love of learning." Phil Lyons, a high school Social Studies teacher, came to much the same conclusion. "Homework," he said, "basically contributes to a situation where students see learning as just an unpleasant means to an end – a way to accrue points." This teacher concluded that trying to improve the quality of homework assignments wouldn't solve the problem, so he finally decided to stop giving homework altogether. According to Kohn, homework simply reinforces what is already a terrible problem in America's archaic educational system: it emphasizes reading because there will be a quiz on the reading, it mandates dozens of identical math problems because the test will contain dozens more just like the ones on the homework and it asks students to respond to end of the chapter questions like "which country did Napoleon invade in 1812?" All of the tasks are time-consuming, dreary, uninspiring, and serve only to kill whatever motivation remains in kids.

"There is no traditional homework at the Bellweather School in Wilson, VT, except when children ask for it or are so excited about a project that they continue to work on it at home," says Marta Beede, the school's top administrator. The Beacon Day School in Oakland, CA Principal Thelma Farly reassures parents that their students do just fine without any homework in terms of both conventional academic achievement and their capacity to learn independently. Students at the Wingra School in Madison, WI "learn through thematic units of study that they help to design," according to director Diane Meier. "We are not a 'practice sheet' kind of school and we do not give homework."

At Cargifield, a school near Edinburgh, Scotland, headmaster John Elder observed that homework made students miserable and rebellious, which in turn slowed their academic progress. Since mandatory assignments have been eliminated, students have "become more responsible for what they choose to study away from school while sparing parents the anguish of having to help their children with intricate problems they themselves barely comprehend." The goal is to help kids think for themselves. One year after instituting the policy, Elder reported "a noticeable difference in the performance of pupils' entrance exams for senior school. Exam marks in maths and sciences have improved by as much as 20%." In my experience as a teacher who gave out very small amounts of homework, many of these assignments dealt with eating dinner with your parents or not watching television for the weekend or picking up a new hobby. My students were allowed to develop an inner life that allowed them to start out on the path of self-knowledge.

One of the sad realities of many of our Islamic schools is that we are creating many students who don't have time for a more balanced life who are stuck in a childish state because most of their waking hours are spent surrounded by people their own age or doing homework or watching TV. I'll leave you with this from John Taylor Gatto, a former New York State Teacher of the Year:

1. Out of 168 hours in each week, my children sleep 56. That leaves then 112 hours a week to fashion a self.

2. My children watch 55 hours of television a week according to recent reports. That leaves them 57 hours a week in school to grow up.

3. My children attend school 30 hours a week, use about 6 hours getting ready, going and coming home, and spend an average of 7 hours a week in homework for a total of 45 hours.

4. During that time, they are under constant surveillance, having no private time or private space and are disciplined if they try to assert individuality in their use of time and space.

5. That leaves 12 hours a week out of which to create a unique consciousness.

6. Of course my kids eat and that takes some time – not much because they've lost the tradition of family dining – but we allot 3 hours a week to eating meals.

7. We arrive at a net amount of private time for each child of 9 hours.

One of the major problems of modern schooling is that it has become so specialized that common sense is often disregarded as being naïve or irresponsible. But a question we as parents and educators need to ask ourselves is are we trying to keep young people busy with homework because we do not really trust what they do with their free time? As one parent stated, "I like it when my kids get homework over the summer. It keeps them out of trouble."

This type of control does nothing but extends childhood and make growing up and handling responsibility difficult for young people today.

Chapter 2

How to Live Religious Studies

through Service Learning

"He who is greatest amongst you shall be your servant."

- *Prophet Jesus (Peace Be Upon Him)*

"The leader's job is to take care of the people."

- *Umar ibn Khattab (RA)*

How to Live Religious Studies through Service Learning

Definition of Service learning

Service Learning is a form of education in which students engage in activities that address human and community needs with structured opportunities intentionally designed to promote student learning and development. Service learning allows students to go into their communities and apply the concepts they have learned in Science, Language Arts, Math, or Economics as well as put them into action. This application of knowledge is key to comprehending the subject at hand.

Service learning as a concept is as old as apprenticeships. Apprenticeships could be called the oldest and most effective form of teaching in history because the teacher taught the students and allowed them to practice the skills whether it is in carpentry, steelwork, or cobble making. Today we call these opportunities internships. Even in education before you can become a certified teacher you have to complete a semester of student-teaching where they applying what you learned to real-life situations and most teachers will testify that they learned more student teaching than they did during 2 or 4 years of coursework.

Goals of Service learning

- To encourage all students to test their academic knowledge in real-life situations by using the community as a classroom.
- To create an atmosphere where community service is not only an extracurricular activity but also a component to a student's intellectual and personal development.
- To create a student presence in the community.
- To increase self-esteem in the students.
- To promote team building among the participants.

In relation to the first goal, when students see that their knowledge base is sound through their own application of it, they begin to build a trust in their teachers as well as in the knowledge. The goal of education is to get students to the level of being critical thinkers. An example of this is a program in the state of Montana where students in middle school and high school were educated in water management and water quality parameters and assessment. They were then allowed to put their knowledge into practice by completing a project called Project Clean Stream Teams, where students removed garbage along frequently used streams. This project attracted press coverage for students with diverse backgrounds. The students received recognition, certificates, and the opportunity to reflect on their work.

The second goal is creating an atmosphere where community service plays an integral role in education. Here are some reflections by students from Perry Meridian High School located in Indianapolis, IN, where students participate in many service learning projects.

- "I can use what I know to help someone else. I feel it has made me a better person and helped me realize I can make a difference." Melissa Meyer
- "Service learning has shown me that you can learn important aspects of life outside of school." Nick Jackson

The third goal of service learning is to create a student presence in the community. It is no secret that schools that have high parental involvement and community support perform better than schools that lack these things. The community ties are strengthened when students seek out the needs of their communities and work to address the issues facing the community. Adults become familiar with students, making neighborhoods stronger because familiarity leads to comfort and a common goal of making the community better. Improving the community can be the first step towards making the country and then the world a better place for everyone. Parents and community members can work with students to achieve these goals.

The fourth and fifth goals are to increase the self-esteem of students and to promote team building. It is human nature to desire to be part of something, especially in the pre-teen and teenage years. This is why young people cherish their friendships and feel the great weight of peer pressure. You can also see this at the university level with the saturation of fraternities, sororities, and various student associations. Service learning can create that group atmosphere in a positive way and encourage youth to learn how to work with others to solve problems.

Purpose of Islamic Studies

One of the purposes of Islamic studies is to teach and generate an understanding of the guidelines and traditions of Islam. We desire that our students become knowledgeable and develop a love for the Prophet Muhammad ((peace and blessings of Allah be upon him). As teachers and parents, we desire that our own students get their dignity and self-esteem from practicing Islam.

Islam is clear about right and wrong and we are commanded to be of those who do good things and benefit humanity.

Service learning and Islamic Studies

A'isha was once asked to describe the Prophet (pbuh), and she replied that he was 'the Quran walking", meaning that his behavior was the Quran translated into action. He applied the Book of Allah to real-life situations. This is what we should desire for ourselves and our children – to make the Book of Allah and the Sunnah of the Prophet (saas) a natural part of our daily lives. This is what service learning does in regards to academic subjects. Service learning allows the students to apply the knowledge of a particular subject to real-life situations. There are many ways in which service learning can also be applied to Islamic Studies. We will examine some ideas that can be implemented immediately and some that would take more time to develop.

One of the most important aspects of the Prophet's (pbuh) life is the importance of taking care of the poor and the needy. Allah reiterates this idea in Surah Al-Ma'oon verses 1-7:

1)   See you one who denies the Judgment (to come)?
2)   Then such is the one who repulses the orphan,
3)   And encourages not the feeding of the indigent.
4)   So woe to the worshippers,
5)   Who are neglectful of their Prayers,
6)   Those who (want but) to be seen,
7)   But refuse (to supply) (even) neighbourly needs.

Service learning Projects in Islamic Schools

Students at all levels of education can participate in service learning. Elementary students could help work on a food drive that would benefit a local shelter to food bank as part of their Islamic Studies curriculum.

The students can create signs promoting the event and decorate boxes that would hold the food being collected. Older students can volunteer their time at homeless shelters, serving food or just talking to people. At a former school I worked at, our middle and high school students organized and hosted a party for small children who lived in a local homeless shelter. Using the drama techniques they learned in Language Arts, they produced a play tailored to the young kids. They also did some face painting along with other fun activities that helped these small children forget about their situations for a little while. Our students became attached to these small children and were deeply touched by the gratitude they showed. As one of them noted in a reflective journal, "On Saturday we all went to a homeless shelter where all these little kids lived. We threw them a party and gave them prizes and gifts. You should have seen the look on their faces. They were so happy, I was going to burst into tears, but I just swallowed them. I've never seen kids that happy...."

Another way to create a strong empathy for the poor is to assist some of the refugees that come to the United States from Muslim majority countries. Many of these refugees come with nothing more than the clothes on their backs. We must begin to help them by focusing and acting up on the many Ayah in the Qur'an and hadith that talk about helping the poor and needy.

A school garden is another way to teach Islamic values. Many of today's youth will never experience the miracle of gardening because we live in places where food is extremely accessible through supermarkets. This activity requires knowledge of Science, hard work, patience, and trust in Allah. The miracle of food is addressed in Surah 'Abasa verses 24-32:

24)   Then let man look at his food, (and how We provide it):
25)   For that We pour forth water in abundance,
26)   And we split the earth in fragments,
27)   And produce therein grain.
28)   And grapes and the fresh vegetation,
29)   And Olives and Dates,
30)   And enclosed gardens, dense with lofty trees,
31)   And fruits and fodder
32)   A provision for you and your cattle.

It is also addressed in Surah Al-An'aam verse 99:

99)   It is He Who sendeth down rain from the skies: with it We produce vegetation of all kinds: from some We produce green (crops), out of which We produce, close-compounded grains out of the date-palm and its sheath (or spathes) (come) clusters of dates hanging low and near: and (then there are) gardens of grapes and pomegranates, each similar (in kind) yet different (in variety): when they begin to bear fruit, feast your eyes with

the fruit and ripeness thereof. Behold!
In these things are Signs for people who
believe.

Another easy-to-implement service learning project

addresses the rights of the neighbor. The Prophet

Muhammad (pbuh) said "Whosoever believes in Allah

and the last day should treat his neighbor kindly."

(Muslim) We must instill in our students the necessity

of treating the neighbors of our schools kindly by

visiting them and taking them gifts. This could

remove some of the animosity they may have in their

hearts towards Muslims because they may never have

met a Muslim before. This also gives our students the

opportunity to internalize a major aspect of Islam and

allow them to represent the best of their religion.

Particularly in this time when a majority of Americans

have a negative view of Islam, partly due to the lack of

personal experience with Muslims. The responsibility

falls on Muslims due to the religious injunctions to serve one's neighbors.

Some other service learning projects require more planning. Students could contact local nursing homes and hospitals about volunteering to visit the sick and the elderly. Camping trips for students can be planned since many students live in cities and suburbs where they cannot fully appreciate Allah's Creations in a natural setting. On the campouts, students can witness the beauty of the stars and see how important and miraculous the ability to create fire is, they will appreciate the Blessings Allah Bestows on us daily. There will be no TV's or radios around to distract them from this reflection. Students could also visit farms, where the Greatness and Wisdom and Allah are also displayed. Milking a cow may help the students gain a better understanding of Surah An-Nahl verse 66:

66)   And most surely there is a lesson for you in the cattle; We give you to drink of what is in their bellies – from betwixt, the feces and the blood – pure milk, easy and agreeable to swallow for those who drink.

Students could also organize night of appreciation where they plan a program, including food and gifts, to show honor and respect to their parents, a major commandment in Islam. I have been a part of this type of program at a couple of different schools and this always works well. Parents get into the routine of dropping their kids off at school or coming to a fundraiser, so this parent program is a pleasant change and builds relationships among parents, which builds communities and bonds of brotherhood and sisterhood.

Benefits of Service Learning

The benefits of teaching Islamic Studies with a service learning format are numerous. Your school will be a haven of good deeds so, insha'Allah, the school as a whole will be rewarded. Students also will have the opportunity to serve mankind and reflect on the power and responsibility of that service. Connecting our Muslim youth with their communities helps enhance dawah efforts and acceptance of Muslims as good people in the dominant society. You help shape young people who will continue to strive to make the world better for all mankind. You enhance cross-curriculum work that incorporates Math, Language Arts, and Science in projects. Islamic schools and Islamic Studies will become fun, interesting, and hands-on. Currently, many students find Islamic Studies boring and irrelevant. As Seth Godin states in his book The Purple Cow, "If a product's future is unlikely to be remarkable- if you can't imagine a future in which people are once again fascinated by your product- it's time to realize that the game has changed. Instead of investing in a dying product, take profits and reinvest them in building something new. "

More Service learning information

In 1990, the Corporation for National and Community Service Learning said that service learning:

- Promotes learning through active participation in service experience

- Promotes structured time for students to reflect by thinking, discussing, and/or writing about their service experience

- Provides an opportunity for students to use skills and knowledge in real-life situations

- Fosters a sense of caring for others

- Extends learning beyond the classroom and into the community

According to the National Commission on Service Learning, service learning:

- Links to academic content and standards

- Involves young people in helping to determine and meet real-life community needs

- Is reciprocal in nature, benefitting both the community and the service provider

- Can be used in any subject area as long as it is appropriate to the learning goal

- Works at all ages, even among young children

Service learning is NOT:

- An episodic volunteer program

- An add-on to an existing school curriculum

- Logging onto a set number of community service hours to graduate

- Compensatory service assigned as a form of punishment by the courts or by school administrators

- Only for high school or college students

- One-sided: benefitting only the students or only the community

"Service learning can be so much fun I forget I'm doing schoolwork and actually learning. Service learning is great for everyone because it gives you skills for life. You learn leadership skills, get a better self-esteem, and help your community, all at the same time." – Common Day student

"Service learning addresses three major issues in education – relevance of the curriculum, level of rigor, and relationships. It is about hope, inspiration, and learning for kids." – Rudy Crew, former Chancellor of New York City Schools

"Be the change you want to see in the world." – Gandhi

"I wish adults would understand that students have innovations, mind-boggling ideas, and that students can put those ideas into action. They can make the world a better place." – June 17 T.N.

"Service is the rent we pay for living." – Marian Wright Edelman

"Everyone wants to do something that matters. When I was in high school, everyone talked about the 'real world' and how we could achieve in the 'real world' after high school. Service learning got us involved in the real world while we were still in high school. It let us do things that were important and let us see that what we were learning was important to solving real world problems." – Student, MIT

"Service learning resurrects idealism, compassion, and altruism…we cannot survive as a nation unless we hold onto these qualities and teach them to our children." – Madeleine Kunin, former Deputy, US Department of Education

"Our community believes that high stakes testing and student achievement are important. As a community, we also want to work on leadership, character, and civic development. Service learning lets us do it all." – Beverly Holt, Senior Coordinator

Summary

Service learning is that "something new" that could be incorporated into an Islamic Studies curriculum. According to an article in *Blueprint* magazine, "the two traditional methods used to convey information in American schools are visual and auditory. These two leave out the kinesthetic learners – the 10% of the population that learns hands-on." Religious instruction cannot afford to leave anyone out. Another benefit of running a service learning program is the possibility of bringing back the alumni as mentors for some of these projects. This also sets the standard for what being an alumnus of your school means, giving back to the school and the community, even after graduation.

Volunteer Organizations and Opportunities

- Local Volunteer Centers

- Red Cross

- United Way

- Habitat for Humanity

- Local Senior Citizens Centers

- Children's Hospitals

- 4H Club – Agriculture and Gardening

- March of Dimes – Diabetes Awareness

- St. Jude Children's Hospital – Cancer Research and Treatment

- Homeless Shelters and Soup Kitchens

- Neighbors – Those Close To Your Homes And Schools

Chapter 3

Curriculum Mapping

Curriculum Mapping

Imagine yourself in a major city here in the U.S. It's late at night and you are looking for your hotel. You're sitting in your rental car looking for that map they gave you at the counter only to remember you left it on the counter. So, you're lost looking for a Motel 6, hoping they left the light on for you. This is the equivalent of a small charter, parochial, or private school going into the field of education without a curriculum map.

What is Curriculum Mapping?

Curriculum mapping is the means by which a school decides within a particular

discipline what will be taught, in what sequence, how it will assessed and what some of the best practices in teaching the subject matter may

be. What is commonplace amongst small charter,

private, or parochial schools is that you have individual

teachers creating his or her own plan for the year,

which takes from precious planning time. So the

proverbial snowball starts rolling. The area next

affected by this are the students because they benefit

from a good presentation of the material. Then the

parents suffer because their child is struggling to do

their homework, which is already taking away from

family time. In a lot of cases the parent cannot help the

child with his or her homework. The last group to be

affected will be the board members and administrators

who are the people that can alleviate the problem by

insisting that the school operate with curriculum maps.

Function of Curriculum Mapping

Curriculum maps operate in three functions. The first

is communication. If at any

time the parents want to know where the students are

in terms of learning they are able to

do so by looking at the map. For example, if you have

a new parent and they inquire as

to what the students are learning or have learned up to

this point it is very easy to show them. This eliminates

the disorganization that many small schools are

accused of because they don't have the organizational

structure that larger districts have. Curriculum maps

also serve as communication between teachers as well.

Cross-curriculum opportunities are abundant when

teachers know at the beginning of the school year

generally where they are going to be at a specific point

in the school year. So if the History teacher is going to

be teaching WWII in January and the Language Arts teacher knows this, he or she can choose a text that can assist the History instructor instead of him/her trying to shove a lot of different types of information on the students. For example, the Language Arts instructor could choose the book *The Diary of Anne Frank,* which would coincide with the time frame the History teacher is teaching. This would assist both instructors in the sense that the students would already have background information. This makes teaching easier while at the same time building a feeling of teamwork amongst the staff. This is always a positive thing, as the late President Lyndon Johnson said, "There are no problems we cannot solve together and very few that we can solve by ourselves." It also serves as a means of communicating with the students. Students are more comfortable when there is a plan of action and they know there is a goal. Then their attitude is one of assuredness and, in education as well as in life, attitude is the difference between success and failure. As author J. Sidlow Baxter wrote, "What is the difference between an obstacle and an opportunity? Our attitude towards it. Every opportunity has a difficulty and every difficulty has an opportunity."

The second function of curriculum maps is to give the meat and potatoes of instruction. These involve Content, Skills, Best Practices, and Assessment tools. Content is what information will be taught. Skills are the necessary tools that are needed to achieve what is being taught and what the student will have after the information is taught. Best practices are what have been found to be the best way to teach material, where the information is processed by the student at a greater capacity. Assessment is the means by which competency is measured. This is the way the student will show what he/she has learned.

The third function of curriculum maps is organization of the school year. Teachers plan a student-centered curriculum. Curriculum maps are flexible and can be modified according to students' strengths and weaknesses. Any education that is not student-centered is not education. One of the things that parents who are looking for a school to put their child in talk about is how well organized it seems. What school leaders need to remember is that parents are entrusting us with their most prized possession - their children. This is a great responsibility and needs to be taken seriously. In a broader sense, schools seem to know that they need a vision. The same is true in the classroom.

Benefits of Curriculum Mapping

The benefits of curriculum mapping are many, however I will highlight three. The first benefit is structure. Without structure, no building, purpose, organization, or human being will be successful. Curriculum maps give a structure for what is going to be taught, when it will be taught, and in what sequence it will be taught. This gives a structural base from which everything else can flow. Every instructor would have a blueprint to work from and would know exactly what is expected from him or her. People perform better when they know what is expected from them.

The second benefit is flexibility. Curriculum maps are living documents that can be changed and modified to fit the students. One of the hallmarks of a good classroom is that it is flexible. You cannot deal with 20-30 people and expect it to always go as planned. Having a curriculum map doesn't mean that everything has to be covered; it is the goal of what you want to accomplish. "A people with no vision will perish."

The last benefit is knowing the best practices in conveying the information. Teaching has been around for thousands of years. Using those practices that have been the most successful is essential to success as a teacher and an institution. Education has become the one area where we have disregarded its history. When we were producing people who created the sciences, mathematics, philosophy, and psychology, we were using best practices. We have to get back to our roots and study and implement those practices that have been time tested and approved. You can't do that if you are scrambling everyday trying to figure out what you are going to teach and what method you are going to use to teach it.

Summary

In summary, curriculum mapping is an essential tool in the creation and sustainability of any good educational institution. It gives the school credibility through organization, teamwork, structure, student-driven and centered curriculum, and flexibility. The process of curriculum mapping involves the staff and administration with the student in mind. The state and accreditation standards are gathered and evaluated along with the material on hand in order to effectively create a curriculum map that fits not only the subject but the institution as well.

Chapter 4

Why Parenting Classes are a

Necessity

"It takes a village to raise a child."
African Proverb

Why Parenting Classes are a Necessity

The Need for Parenting Workshops in Islamic Schools

Parental Involvement has been a buzzword in the world of education lately now more than ever before in the history of American education. Schools are pushing parents to be involved in their children's academic lives so that they can achieve more. Islamic schools have also jumped on this bandwagon; however the need is not so much on academics but on the social, spiritual and mental development of their children.

Because of this, there is a need for our Islamic schools and community centers to provide parenting classes to give parents some strategies to assist them in combating the negative messages that are anti-family and anti-religious ethics that our society sends. Many parents can't recognize these dangers and only focus on the academic development of their child while many children can be doing well academically but socially they can be struggling. Another issue that parents may not understand is how to navigate the American teenage world. Due to the extension of adolescence it is hard for parents to understand what their child is going through or who is influencing their child because the teenage years have become like a culture unto itself. This can be seen recently in Toronto with the story of the young lady Aqsa Parvez who was killed by her father after having conflicts concerning dress, behavior, and Allah knows best what else. This story shows us that there is a need to reevaluate and educate our parents on how to handle issues like the strong-willed child versus the compliant child, listening to our children instead of the children should be seen and not heard approach, how children are given a message of their individuality instead of a commitment to a group/family on a daily basis, and music, Facebook and dating. All of these issues affect the children who are sitting in our schools and in order to really educate the whole child we must address them. This also bridges the gap between school and the parents where both parties can be on the same page, which is beneficial for all parties.

The laser-like focus on academics has been very successful on getting our number of doctors, engineers, and lawyers. However, the downside of this is the de-emphasis on character and conduct. There used to be a time where next to the academic grades there were citizenship grades. These citizenship grades were not only a reflection of the child but on the family itself. Now those citizenship grades are not as important not only in the public school realm but also in our Islamic schools. Some of this can be traced back to parents, teachers, and administrators worrying about how children feel (self-esteem) rather than self-respect. This problem is played out every day in schools where students disrespect their fellow classmates, teachers, and administrators, all because for their entire lives, people wanted to make their loves easier instead of making them respect those in charge and their elders. As Jill Rigby states in her book <u>Raising Disrespectful Children in a Disrespectful World</u>, "As a result of this emphasis on self-esteem, twenty-somethings are returning home rather than facing the world on their own. College kids are flunking out because they don't know how to manage their schedules. Kids are growing up without problem-solving skills because their parents think love means solving all their problems for them. Many adolescents have no respect for authority because their parents didn't command their respect. Instead, their parents gave too much and exposed them to too little. In our attempt to build self-esteem in children, we have reared a generation of young people who are failing at life, haven't a clue who they are, and are struggling to find a reason for living. Their kids fall for the latest craze, healthy or unhealthy. It doesn't matter, as long as they are in the middle of it. They would rather die than give up their cell phones. And they feel that others have an obligation to serve them."

If you look at a chart with the results of the 2 parenting goals:

Self- Esteem	Self-Respect
• Happiness	• Joyful
• Greed	• Humble
• Arrogance	• Confident
• Insecurity	• Good Manners

• Bad Manners	• Altruism
• Selfish	

Many of our teachers have to deal with students who have bad manners and when they do write up these students and have a parent-teacher conference, the parent begins to blame the teacher. I know this because I've had this experience in both my public and Islamic school teaching days. On one occasion, I met with a parent of a student who had a particularly foul mouth and was quite disrespectful to others. This student's father came into a meeting instructing a group of teachers how we could tech more so that his child could do better. This left us perplexed and wondering what the meeting was about.

As a community we are in danger from this for a couple of reasons. One reason is that many of our students come from families who are first generation in

American. With this comes many challenges but the one pertinent to this discussion is the guilt that many parents feel living in America. This guilt come out in trying to overcompensate and make the kids happy because they realize their kids are missing out on family and culture. This compensation usually comes in the material realm and giving them whatever they need. The thing that the child is expected to give in return in the good grades which will last probably until school gets tough and they no longer want to work hard. Because they will never have had to do anything difficult, they won't be able to fight through it.

Another problem is the hierarchy in the home. Many of our students don't respect men or dad because the child is the center of attention because with many of our homes, the paradigm is off. In a home where character is the #1 priority, the hierarchy is:

God

Spouse

Children

Community

Self

This reinforces to children that they were born into the family that is loving and already has a set order of rules. The husband respects and honors the wife and the wife honors and respects the husband and the children fall in line.

Another problem that can be helped with parenting classes is the teenage years. In America, we've created a whole new culture that has its own language, dress, food, and norms. This culture, popular culture, can be very difficult for parents to deal with because it's different from other traditional cultures and it changes rapidly. Traditional cultures have set norms in terms of dress, food, and behavior that have lasted for hundreds and even thousands of years. When people don't feel like they are part of a tribe, group, or family, they normally join the dominant group. When you have parents that come from a very traditional society, this can be a source of conflict.

- Estimated number of American homes with televisions – 109.6 million
- Average time American kids spend watching television every day – 4 hours
- Before the age of 18. the average child will witness over 200,000 acts of violence on television, including 16,000 murders
- 83% of the episodes of the top 20 shows among teen viewers contained some sexual content including 20% with sexual intercourse

- The video game "Grand Theft Auto: Vice City" rated M (Mature), was the bestselling video game among teens and pre-teens. In it, players can simulate having sex with a prostitute and then killing her.

The teenage years can be very intimidating for parents as the child begins to develop his or her own identity and friendships. Also, parents themselves begin to feel old, which was traditionally a good thing. But in modern-day society, those who are older are seen as less intelligent or not hip. This is the time where the individualism of our society becomes evident. Many teens begin to feel that they are not part of a family unit but that their friends are more important than their family. This is why parents must know who their children are taking on as friends. This is also why it very important for parents to talk to their teens and go into their children's world in a non-judgmental way. With this approach, children will be given the right answer from people who care about them, not from "friends" who are their age and who have no life experience. Many families are losing their children to this teenage culture because they won't/can't talk to your children about your family expectations and where their child fits into this. If parents look at why friends are so important to all of us; it generally boils down to a point John Maxwell

notes in his book <u>Winning With People</u>:

1. Everybody wants to be somebody. Our kids want to matter if they don't

   feel valued by us, they will feel valued by "friends."

2. Nobody cares how much you know until he knows how much you care.

In parenting and in teaching, those under you have to think you care about

> them in order to do things they may not
>
> understand why.

3. Everybody needs somebody. People sometimes have trouble with having confidence in themselves. So they need a good support system.

4. Anybody that helps somebody influences lots of bodies. With teenagers, influence is far more powerful than control, you can't control a teenager and they will do things to show you that they can't be controlled.

5. Somebody today will rise up and become somebody.

Parents also need training in how to handle the Skype, Twitter, Facebook, music, dating, cell phones, and other popular culture themes. Many parents don't know what these things are, much less the damage and influence that these have on their children. As David Elkind states in The Hurried Child, "Therefore, one consequence to children of television homogenization and the decade long swings between fantasy and reality is to create what we might be called pseudo-sophistication. School age children today know much more than they understand. They are able to talk about nuclear fission, tube worms at 20,000 fathoms, space shuttles, chat rooms, and surfing the net." If parents don't sit their children down and talk to them about these subjects, there will be real issues. However, if parents are not knowledgeable then children don't take them seriously. Especially in our current society where on television the father is seen as an idiot and the mother and children basically have to work around his stupidity. There is a subtle message in doing this that goes to attacking the head of

the household and parents need to

be made aware of this.

The teenage years in America have become, as one

gentleman put it plainly, a time period where people

make excuses for bad behavior. According to Imam

Ali (RA), he said during the years from ages 14-21,

which we consider the bulk of the teenage years; you

should befriend your child at this age group. When

young people have their parents as their friends, they

go to them for advice, want to spend time with them,

and want to emulate them. This time period in a young

person's life is difficult for the child but also the

parent. Some of the reasons why it is difficult for the

child are: puberty, which leads to hormonal and

physical changes, the need for their own identity, and

wanting more freedom. For the adult, this is a difficult age because of the following

reason: the adult is recognizing that they are getting older, which makes them sometimes want to exert more control over their child in a quest to stop the clock. This leads to the same battle they had with the child when the child was 2-3 years old. It's about releasing control. Releasing control is very difficult, especially for many parents in our community because they feel like they have to control what their children are experiencing.

Summary

In conclusion, many parents trust our Islamic schools with their most prized possessions – their children. We who are seen as having expertise have a duty not only to put our children in the best possible position to be successful but to also educate their parents, who are in most cases not knowledgeable about the educational system or society within which their child is growing up in. As John Taylor Gatto states in his book <u>A Different Kind of Teacher</u>, "A lot of my kids don't like their families very much either. One of our eighth graders murdered his parents last May for the insurance money. He was thirteen or fourteen (and there wasn't any insurance money) but he saw a murder like that on television and figured everyone had insurance who wasn't a kid. That's an awful thing to say but his disaffection of families is built into the way we school- shutting parents out of the important rooms of their own kids' lives."

Now this may sound far-fetched for Islamic schools,
but in my experience as a teacher and parent at a
couple of different Islamic schools, the amount of
pressure, anxiety, and angst between families is
enough to make me say that parenting workshops are a
must at our Islamic schools, centers, and masjids. As
our Prophet (saas) said: "The best thing a parent can
give a child is good character." In order for a parent to
embark on this quest of giving their child good
character, they need to know those obstacles in the
society that may hinder parents in cultivating that
character.

One may say that our religious institutions should be
teaching these classes instead of a school. This
argument does hold some weight; however, schools
have an added interest in the fact that if parents get on
board, then the school climate improves. Also, the

classes that come out of the school could eventually benefit the broader community. Parenting is too hard a job for two people to do. If parents try to do it on their own and fail, then we all lose.

Chapter 5

Leadership

"Everything begins and ends with leadership."

- *John Maxwell*

"The first responsibility of a leader is to define

reality."

– *Max Depree*

Leadership

How do you pick a leader, or in a school's case, a principal or headmaster? Every year, hundreds, if not thousands, of schools are facing this dilemma. Part of the reason is because they did not get it right the first time. The first step in picking a good leader is to collectively come up with a list of skills and talents that you liked and disliked in the leader who just left. The second step is to look at the vision statement of the school and what skills are essential in attaining the vision. This allows the hiring committee to begin to prioritize the skills that candidates have. For example, let's say a school's priority is to recruit 50-75 new students in the next 5 years as well as increase test scores. After interviewing numerous candidates, they narrow it down to 2. Both of these candidates speak

81

well, have knowledge of pedagogy, and have advanced education degrees. However, one of them went to public school and has more experience in community involvement than the other. This attribute opens the door for recruiting more students because the one with more interaction with the community probably has more experience in building relationships.

John Maxwell states, "People don't care how much you know until they know how much you care." At their core, relationships are about someone caring for another person, not necessarily two people caring about each other at its inception. For example, mothers love and care for their children far before the time it becomes reciprocal. Teachers go into teaching because they care for children. Not one child in particular, but children in general. This generality becomes manifested in particulars when the person becomes a teacher. This can be seen in the term used for a graduate of a school or university, "alma mater", which means the nurturing mother. Schools are more than grades and test scores, they are utilitarian relationships in the sense that the student uses the school to get into a good college and the school uses the test scores to gain more students. The trouble with this model is that there are thousands of schools that use this model. Often the result of using this model is alumni who never come back to visit the school because they feel they got what they were supposed to get and that the relationship is over. Have you ever gone back to school to see a principal or a teacher who really touched your heart and soul? Was this connection based on test scores and grades or someone caring for you before you cared for them? As the saying goes, hearts are inclined to people who treat them well.

All of this has to come into consideration when hiring your leaders as well as your staff. Do they have the skills to help in attaining your vision? This saves schools time, money, and heartache because when you don't keep your vision in mind, you will inevitably spend more money hiring and firing. Time lost when you divert from your vision statement can never be regained. Heartache comes when you have developed relationships and you realize they do not fit into the organization's vision.

Not everyone on your team can take the journey to where you are taking the school. John Maxwell, in his book <u>Teamwork 101</u>, gives some characteristics of people who can't take the journey:

- They won't work on personal weaknesses

- They can't keep up with other team members

- They don't grow in their area of responsibility

- They won't work with the rest of the team

Many times, schools will keep people around who display these characteristics because it is convenient or they are liked. However, doing this jeopardizes the whole team because the level of expectation among the team goes down.

How do I build and keep a staff that will reach the vision?

Retention rates for teachers and students in private schools are problematic at best. There are many reasons for this – low pay, overbearing principals, long hours, etc. In many schools towards the end of the year there is always some fear that the best teachers may not be coming back. I would like to offer a few suggestions for this situation:

1. Commit resources to develop your staff. When people feel like they are growing in an organization, it is very difficult to leave.

2. Look for potential leaders.

People feel more connected to a project if you allow them to take lead of programs. Sometimes principals can stifle their most talented staff members by having them work on menial committees or groups that are not in their strength zone. This often does one of two things. They either get frustrated enough to do only minimum work or they get pushed right out of the door. In his book Teamwork 101, John Maxwell gives some characteristics of potential leaders:

1. They make things happen

2. They see opportunities

3. They influence the opinion and actions of others

4. They add value to you

5. They provide ideas that help the organization

It is important to recognize the potential leaders because if you don't, these people will find a place to fly their ideas. As Pulitzer Prize-winning historian Garry Willis said, "Leaders have a say in what they are being led to." Due to the fact that many school leaders are from the same colleges of education as those who were at failing schools, what you find is an absence of ideas because they are so degree-focused instead of leader-focused. For the most part, leaders are not made in colleges of education. They receive their theoretical training there, but not those skills or inherent qualities that make someone a leader. In my own experience, I have worked with people who had the formal training and those intangible qualities that leaders need, but were looked over for leadership positions.

What about the employee who is unorthodox but effective?

On almost every job, there is someone who seems to do things in a quirky or unorthodox kind of way and they get results. However, to some people on the outside, this may seem like an undisciplined type of teacher or administrator. Oftentimes, particular in education, we get used to cookie cutter programs or doing things the way we were taught, or what Yale, Harvard, or the NEA is saying to use as a barometer of what normal is. We forget that the most important thing a leader is responsible for is results. Leadership expert Peter Drucker said, "effective leadership is not about making speeches or being liked, it is defined by results, not attributes." These employees need to be protected by those who are in the position to protect them (i.e. principals, board members, parents, and community leaders). If these employees are not protected, they may be run out of the organization by someone who will realize years later what a great asset they were. If a school wants to be successful, it will need to have a leader who is a visionary with courage to be able to withstand criticism. People often do not

understand new ideas, particularly in education.

People get degrees from teacher colleges that often

produce the same "group think" mentality that created

many of the underlying problems in education.

Chapter 6

Creating a Natural School Environment

"Learning is like breathing. It is a natural, human activity; it is part of being alive…Our ability to learn, like our ability to breathe, does not need to be improved or tampered with. All that is needed is an interesting, accessible, intelligible world, and a chance to play a meaningful part in it."

- Aaron Falbel

Creating a Natural School Environment

In his marketing book The Purple Cow, Seth Godin speaks of how to make your business one that is remarkable. So what are the essentials of a "purple school"? What does a remarkable school look like? What type of students does it produce? Is there a way to "measure" student progress? And if we recognize that the current model of education is not good, then why do we just keep creating safe, ordinary schools and combine them with great marketing? You cannot drive down the street of any major city and not see numerous billboards for charter schools, districts that advertise test scores or low student-teacher ratios. None of these advertisements promote one of the most important ingredients to success, which is a passion for success. Below I have listed 5 things a "purple school" (remarkable school) should have.

1. **Service Learning** – Dr. Martin Luther King Jr. stated that "Everybody can be great because everybody can serve." One of the hallmarks of learning is learning what your duty is to your community and how the skills you have, including your youthful energy, can best serve to make the world a better place. This sense of duty helps to cultivate social intelligence where you learn to work with people of different age groups.

2. **Apprenticeships** – Traditionally, if you wanted to be something (i.e. carpenter, cobbler, plumber, teacher), you were apprenticed out to a master teacher of that field. This meant that

you watched them do something, they taught you how to do it, and then they watched you do it over a period until they felt you had mastered the craft. 70% of people are kinetic learners, meaning they learn something through hands-on application. Many of our students, particularly our young men, could benefit from this greatly.

3. **Times of Solitude** – How can a young person truly have self-knowledge if all of their time is spent either going somewhere, looking forward to going somewhere, or thinking about where they just came from? School does not help quell this problem due to the nature of school bells. Many of our students never have time to reflect on what they just learned, or keep that debate going, or finish that thought because in

many ways they were trained that nothing is worth finishing and that we must constantly be moving. In some Japanese schools, students are given time after class to reflect on what they were just taught. If students don't have time to reflect on what they learned beyond surface level, can we assume the understanding of the information?

Even greater than the opportunity to understand information is the opportunity to understand oneself. Probably the greatest thing a person can learn is their own strengths and weaknesses, fears, character flaws, character qualities, future goals, and fondest memories. In order for a school to really teach a child holistically, it must allow for times of solitude, which allows student time to get to know themselves. People who know themselves are far more likely to reach the traditional purpose of education, a word that comes from the Latin work "educare", which means to bring out what is in the individual. This is a different approach than assembly line education, which is what most schools are doing now. Dr. Martin Luther King Jr. once stated that "If a man has not found something worth dying for, then he isn't fit to live." In this modern day experience of life, where there are more distractions now than anytime in human history, how could a person find something he commits himself to so much that he is willing to die for it? Educational institutions have to help our young people find this calling by having time for contemplation, reflection, or just time to do nothing. We are human beings, not human doings.

4. **No homework** – In his lecture "Using Time or Abusing Time", leadership expert John C. Maxwell discusses time management, stating that it is not about time management, it's about priority management. What are those things that should be of priority in the classroom? There are questions a school should ask: Why are we giving the homework? Objective? Are we infringing on the rights of the family to spend time together and be able to teach their child some things about life (i.e. cooking, hobbies, etc.)? Or time they would like to spend as a family?

When giving a description of people who abuse time, Maxwell points out a couple of things that schools do:

- They do things without thinking and this causes wasted time and energy.

- They do things that other want them to do which takes away their uniqueness. Many teachers give homework because the parents pressure them.

- They do things that are not important. This keeps them from being effective. The great writer Henry David Thoreau said, "It is not enough to be busy, the question if what are we busy about." Instead of trying to teach everything lightly, teachers should teach some things deeply. This cuts down on homework and wasted time by the teacher. The child could be using this time to play sports, explore a hobby, talk to their family, etc.

If these things don't convince you, go back and read the chapter on homework.

5. **Playtime** - Children up to the age of 7 should do a lot of playing. In the Islamic tradition, the lives of children are broken down into 7's. The first 7 years are for playing, the next 7 years are for teaching, the next 7 years are for befriending, and then you let them go at 21.

So why is play so important? For those of you who have children or have ever played games with children, when you tell a child "we're going to play a game", one of the first things a child will want to know is what the rules are. After learning rules and boundaries, kids understand that in order to have fun and to be able to continue play, they have to not only keep themselves within the boundaries but also maintain them with other players. In a recent article titled, "Want to get your kids into college? Let them play", Erika Christakis and Nicholas Christakis, a professor of medicine and sociology at Harvard, reinforce this concept by stating that "one of the best predictors of school success is the ability to control impulses." They also say, "Through play, children learn to take turns, delay gratification, negotiate conflicts, solve problems, share goals, acquire flexibility, and live with disappointment." What children learn through playing is another form of intelligence that has been getting a lot of attention lately –

social and emotional intelligence, which allows

students to understand how to get along with

others and where they themselves stand in a

society in regards to duties and responsibilities.

As the Christakis so brilliantly put it at the end

of their article, "…academic achievement in

college requires readiness skills that transcend

mere book learning. It requires the ability to

engage actively with people and ideas. In

short, it requires a deep connection to the

world. For a five-year old, this connection

begins and ends with the creating, questioning,

imitating, dreaming, and sharing that

characterizes play. When we deny young

children play, we are denying them the right to

understand the world. By the time they get to

college, we will have denied them the

opportunity to fix the world too." The latest craze of college prep kindergartens and testing to get kids into private pre-schools and the sort is really sad. It put pressure on young children who should be able to enjoy the world, often causing anxiety and depression.

6. **Stop Testing or Put Testing into Perspective**– Have the courage to stop the testing madness. In his book The Hurried Child, David Elkind gives a brief history of standardized testing. He states that standardized tests were first introduced around the turn of the century by French psychologist Alfred Binet and his colleague Henri Simon. Binet had been commissioned by the French government to find a way to identify mentally retarded children at an early age so they could

be placed in special institutions. To develop his test, Binet went to teachers and asked to describe the sorts of skills they had observed in children of different ages. On the basis of these teacher comments, Binet constructed his test items, which dealt with language, understanding, reasoning, and motor skills. Intelligence testing was useful in screening retarded children, but Binet was very aware of the danger associated with the tests, stating "we should at least spare from this mark (a test score that would send a child to an institution for the retarded) those who do not deserve it. Mistakes are excusable, especially at the beginning. But if they become to gross, we can injure the name of these institutions. Not to mention the costs to the children involved." Unfortunately, Binet's hope was not realized and, as we shall see, we are still making mistakes with tests. If the creator of the standard test was worried about stigmatizing young people for the rest if their lives, what can we say about those who have witnessed his fear come to fruition and did nothing to change it?

References

Crain, William. (2003). *Reclaiming Childhood: Letting Children Be Children in Our Achievement Oriented Society.* New York: Henry Holt and Company.

Elkind, David. (2001). *The Hurried Child.* Cambridge: Perseus Publishing.

Gatto, John Taylor. (2002). *A Different Kind of Teacher.* California: Berkeley Hills Books.

Kohn, Alfie. (2006). *The Homework Myth: Why Our Kids Get Too Much of a Bad Thing.* De Capo Press.

Kralovec, Etta, and John Buell. (2000). *The End of Homework: How Homework Disrupts Families, Overburdens Children, and Limits Learning.* Boston: Beacon Press.

Ohanian, Susan. (2002). *What Happened to Recess and Why are Our Children Struggling in Kindergarten?* McGraw-Hill.

Maxwell, John C. (2003). *Real Leadership: the 101 Collection.* Nashville: Thomas Nelson, Inc.

Mamen, Maggie. (2004). *The Pampered Child Syndrome.* Canada: Creative Bound International Inc., 2004.

Maxwell, John. (2004). *Winning With People.*

Nashville: Thomas Nelson Inc.

Maxwell, John C. (2008). *Success 101.* Nashville:

Thomas Nelson, Inc.

Rigby, Jill. (2006). *Raising Disrespectful Children in a*

Disrespectful World. Howard

Books, 2006

Wormeli, Rick. (2003). *Day one & beyond: practical*

matters for new middle-level   teachers.

Portland: Stenhouse Publishers.

"Service Learning – Student Reflection." [Online]
(2005)
-http://pmhs.msdpt.k12.in.us/students_activities_servic
elearning_reflections.htm